The BLISSFUL BATH

HANDMADE SOAPS, SCENTS, AND DECORATIVE ACCENTS

Compiled by Dawn Anderson

Martingale™
& COMPANY

The Blissful Bath: Handmade Soaps, Scents, and Decorative Accents

© 2002 Martingale & Company

The credits that appear on page 80 are hereby made a part of this copyright page.

Martingale & Company
20205 144th Avenue NE
Woodinville, WA 98072-8478
www.martingale-pub.com

Printed in Hong Kong
07 06 05 04 03 02   8 7 6 5 4 3 2 1

Library of Congress Cataloging-in-Publication Data
The blissful bath: handmade soaps, scents, and decorative accents / compiled by Dawn Anderson.
     p. cm.
   ISBN #1-56477-443-0
   1. Handicraft. 2. Bathrooms. 3. House furnishings. 4. Soap. 5. Perfumes. I. Anderson, Dawn.
TT880 .B55 2002
745.5–dc21   2002007497

Credits

PRESIDENT: *Nancy J. Martin*
CEO: *Daniel J. Martin*
PUBLISHER: *Jane Hamada*
EDITORIAL DIRECTOR: *Mary V. Green*
MANAGING EDITOR: *Tina Cook*
TECHNICAL EDITOR: *Dawn Anderson*
COPY EDITOR: *Karen Koll*
DESIGN DIRECTOR: *Stan Green*
COVER DESIGNER: *Stan Green*
TEXT DESIGNER: *Trina Stahl*

CONTENTS

INTRODUCTION

With the projects in this book you can create a pleasant, tranquil retreat in your own bath area. Discover a collection of scented soaps and skin-care products that you can make to indulge yourself or create to give as gifts. In addition, find several creative home furnishings projects designed especially for decorating the bathroom.

There are recipes for soap, bath tablets, body lotion, and lip balm. Some

of the recipes provide for variations from the basic recipe. The body lotion recipe offers two variations: mango spice and aloe. The lip balm recipe allows you to customize it by your choice of ingredients, colorings, and flavorings.

To enhance the decor of your bathroom, you can choose from projects such as the daisy shower curtain, an embellished bath mat, trimmed towels, a hand-painted soap dish and tumbler, a beaded wastebasket, and a miniature paint-ed chest, perfect for storing cosmet-ics, hair accessories, or jewelry.

This collection of projects for the bath features a variety of crafting techniques, from sewing, to beading, to painting, to soap crafting. You will find projects for all skill levels. Even a novice crafter can create a designer shower curtain easily from a bed sheet and some decorative appliqués. Or make a batch of lip balm in your microwave!

Fragrant BATH TABLETS

By Amy Jenner

These mix-and-mold disks are made with honey. Dissolve one wafer in your bath for a welcome pick-me-up or wind-down.

Slipping into a warm bath scented with these dissolving bath tablets can leave you feeling either energized or relaxed, depending on your choice of essential oils. The recipe is so fast and easy, you may never buy off-the-shelf bath tablets again.

I made the tablets with five natural skin care ingredients: honey, used for centuries to restore moisture to skin; borax or Dead Sea salts, which soften your water, thereby enhancing the effects of other bath ingredients; sea salt, which heals and energizes; French white clay, used to draw impurities from the skin; and essential oil to add fragrance.

This recipe should not be doubled, as the ingredients must be molded while still warm. Use individual metal or plastic candy molds for shaping the tablets. Heat can mar some plastics, and after one or two pressings, plastic molds may lose their contour.

The tablets have a honey color. The addition of dried material—rose petals, cinnamon, mint—adds subtle color and texture.

Materials

MAKES 6 TABLETS, 1½"–2" EACH

½ cup borax or Dead Sea salts

1½ teaspoons sea salt

1 tablespoon French white clay plus extra for sprinkling

1 teaspoon dried ground herbs or flower petals

Essential oil (see "Aromatherapy Blends," page 7)

⅜ cup honey

YOU'LL ALSO NEED:

Wet and dry measuring cups, measuring spoons, food processor, paper towel, mini saucepan, candy thermometer, wooden spoon, 6 small candy or mini tart molds, teaspoon, toothpick, airtight container

Designer's Tip

Use only one tablet per bath, as the essential oils used in the tablets may irritate the skin if used in larger amounts.

Instructions

NOTE: *Make tablets on a clear, dry day.*

1. **Combine dry ingredients and oil.** Place borax or Dead Sea salts, sea salt, French white clay, dried material, and essential oil in food processor. Pulse several times to blend ingredients. Lay paper towel flat on counter and sprinkle surface with French white clay.

2. **Add honey.** Heat honey in mini saucepan over high heat, using candy thermometer to check temperature. When honey begins to boil, stir continuously with wooden spoon. When temperature reaches 300°, immediately remove honey from heat (illustration A). Pour honey into processor and pulse several times until well blended.

3. **Mold tablets.** Press small amount of mixture into individual candy or mini tart mold and pack firmly using back of teaspoon (illustration B). Unmold immediately onto powdered paper towel, using toothpick to pry tablet free. Repeat process, working quickly while mixture is still warm to make 6 tablets total. Let cure 24 hours. Store tablets flat in airtight container.

A. Stir honey with wooden spoon until temperature reaches 300°.

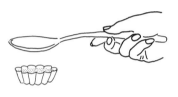

B. Press mixture into candy or tart mold and pack down with back of spoon.

Aromatherapy Blends

TO MAKE SCENTED bath tablets, add any of the following essential oil blends to the six-tablet base recipe.

- **Relaxation:** 16 drops lavender, 13 drops marjoram, 8 drops chamomile, and 8 drops cypress.
- **Romance:** 18 drops sandalwood, 12 drops rosewood, 12 drops ylang-ylang, and 6 drops patchouli.
- **Joy:** 12 drops bergamot, 19 drops orange, and 3 drops basil.
- **Energy:** 9 drops rosemary, 6 drops sweet orange, 3 drops peppermint, and 1 drop thyme.
- **Calm:** 60 drops (1 teaspoon) lavender.

HANDMADE SOAP

By Amy Jenner

Use one basic recipe and my simple technique to create your own special blends of homemade soap. Start with a master "dough" recipe, and then add a variety of ingredients to change the "flavor" of the soap. To create variations on my basic white soap, I add essential oils, fragrance oils, textures, and colorants. You can replicate my tried-and-true soap recipes or create your own special blends.

Soap has three main ingredients: water, chemicals known as alkalis (such as lye), and fats (such as vegetable shortening). The lye is dissolved in water, combined with the fats, and stirred. This activity triggers a chemical reaction called saponification, producing a mixture of soap and glycerin. The natural glycerin found in homemade soap is one of the reasons it is so soothing to the skin. Most commercial soaps do not contain it, as it is removed and sold to other industries. To get started, you need water and lye. Because the various chemical reactions that take place during soap making can be affected by minerals found in hard water, I use rainwater or distilled water. Lye, also known as sodium hydroxide or caustic soda, is available in hardware stores or by mail order from soap-making suppliers. Lye must be used with great caution. Although it is stable when dry, it can cause burns when mixed with water. Always wear safety glasses and rubber gloves. If you should accidentally splash yourself with lye, simply rinse with cool running water.

When the lye is dissolved in water, a chemical reaction takes place, heating the solution up to about 200°. Before you can proceed with the soap-making process, this solution must be cooled to around 95°. In order to cool the lye for soap making, I dissolve it in water the night before.

The soap-making process also requires fat. For my basic recipe, I use vegetable shortening, coconut oil, and olive oil. Each of these oils gives the resulting soap certain properties. Vegetable shortening produces a fine, soft variety of soap. Coconut oil, available at health foods stores (or see Bear America Sales in "Resources," pages 78–79), gives the soap a creamy, thick lather, and olive oil gives it moisturizing qualities.

Before the lye solution and fats are combined, the temperatures of both ingredients need to be brought simultaneously to the same temperature between 95° and 98°. You'll need a pair of meat, dairy, or darkroom thermometers for this process. To prevent false readings, suspend each thermometer with a length of coat hanger in such a way that it doesn't touch the sides or bottom of the container.

Designer's Tip

Before starting the soap-making process, it's worthwhile to check and calibrate your thermometers. To do this, fill a large glass with ice. Add water to the top of the ice and stir. Put both thermometers in the ice bath and keep stirring. They should both read 32°. *Note: Some thermometers are adjustable. After purchasing a new thermometer, I made thirty pounds of bad soap before realizing it was off by 2°.*

Saponification (and constant stirring) give the mixture a creamy, yogurtlike consistency. This is the point at which the soap is "flavored," which is my favorite part of the process. For scent add essential oils or fragrance oil; for color add herbs or spices (e.g., dill, rosemary, cinnamon, clove, or turmeric) or synthetic dyes; and for texture add oatmeal, cornmeal, ground nuts, herbs, or broken flower parts and buds.

In addition to the above ingredients, I add extra olive oil to the soap. This technique, called superfatting, gives the soap added moisturizing qualities. The extra oil becomes suspended in the soap, making it especially rich while at the same time mild enough for use on babies. Once complete, the soap is poured into a mold, allowed to cure, and then cut into bars, squares, or other shapes.

Materials

MAKES ABOUT 8 POUNDS BASIC SOAP

32 ounces rainwater or distilled water

12 ounces lye

38 ounces vegetable shortening

24 ounces coconut oil

24 ounces olive oil, plus 2 ounces for superfatting

4 ounces essential oil or fragrance oil

Herbs, grains, nuts, flowers, spices, and dyes for color and/or texture

YOU'LL ALSO NEED:

2-quart wide-mouth glass jar with cover; kitchen scale (should delineate to the half ounce and go up to 3 pounds); rubber gloves; safety goggles; apron; 2-cup glass measuring cup; 2 basins or sinks; long-handled spoon; newspaper; large cardboard shoebox; small kitchen garbage bag; large insulated picnic cooler; 2 coat hangers; wire cutters; 2 stainless steel or glass meat, dairy, or darkroom thermometers (should measure in the range of 95° to 100° F in 2° delineations); large plastic bowl; 5-quart or larger stainless steel pot; 2 long-handled wooden or stainless steel spoons; small bowl; cutting board; knife; vinegar (for neutralizing lye in case of spill)

Instructions

NOTE: *It is very important in soap making that all measurements are done by weight.*

1. **Mix lye the night before making soap.** Set jar on scale and zero scale to subtract weight of jar. Add rainwater or distilled water to jar until scale reads 32 ounces. Put on gloves, goggles, and apron. Use same method to weigh 12 ounces lye in measuring cup. Set jar with water in sink or basin. Slowly and carefully add lye to water, stir quickly with long-handled spoon to dissolve (avoid breathing fumes), and then cover quickly. Let solution stand overnight.

2. **Set up work area.** On soap-making day, layer newspaper on kitchen counter and floor. Line shoebox with garbage bag; set box in cooler.

3. **Test temperature of lye solution.** Put on gloves, goggles, and apron. Fill sink or basin with hot water to 4" level, set lye jar in it, and remove cover. Bend coat hanger into holder shape and use it to suspend thermometer in lye solution so that thermometer does not touch sides of container (illustration A). Use wire cutters if necessary. Stir lye while checking thermometer reading periodically until final temperature reads between 95° and 98°.

4. **Melt fats.** Weigh 38 ounces shortening in large plastic bowl using method from step 1. Place shortening in pot and heat on low setting until melted; remove from heat. Using same technique, weigh and stir in 24 ounces coconut oil. Once coconut oil is melted, weigh and stir in 24 ounces olive oil. During final stirring, test temperature, making a wire holder as in step 3 to suspend thermometer away from sides of pot. While being stirred, the fat's temperature should read between 95° and 98°. To lower temperature, set pot in sink or basin with cool water bath. To raise temperature, set pot in hot water bath.

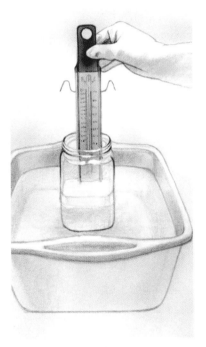

A. Suspend thermometer from coat hanger holder to check the temperature.

B. Melt the fats in a large pot; then add the lye.

5. **Combine lye and fats.** Continue adjusting both temperatures until they match exactly within the 95°–98° range (e.g., both read 97°). Set pot with fats into empty sink or basin and put on gloves, apron, and goggles. Slowly pour lye solution into fats and stir immediately with long-handled spoon (illustration B). Stir until solution takes on thicker, creamier quality, at least 10 minutes.

6. **Add fragrance, colorant, texture, and superfat.** Weigh 4 ounces of essential or fragrance oil and add to soap mixture. To add color or texture, remove 2 cups soap to small bowl and mix in colorant or textural ingredients. If using synthetic dye, follow manufacturer's directions. Mix colored and/or textured soap back into main pot. Stir until mixture takes on a light puddinglike consistency; then weigh and stir in 2 additional ounces of olive oil.

NOTE: *Some essential oils act as a catalyst to saponification, making the soap thicken quickly. This is especially true with the spice essential oils such as bay.*

7. **Mold and cure soap.** Pour mixture into shoebox (illustration C), close lid of cooler, and let soap cure 18 to 24 hours. Unmold finished soap onto cutting board. Turn upright and scrape soda ash from surface with knife. Cut block into cubes, bars, or sticks or hand-mold into balls as desired (illustration D).

C. To mold the soap, pour it into a shoebox within a cooler.

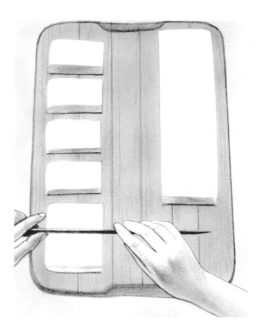

D. Cut the soap block into individual bars.

Variations on the Basic Recipe

Lavender: This mild, creamy white soap makes a good antibacterial soap for children. Add:

4 ounces lavender essential oil

Small handful of lavender buds

Bay spice: A beautiful, dark brown, speckled variety. Add:

2 ounces bay essential oil

1 1/2 ounces cinnamon essential oil

1/2 ounce clove essential oil

1 tablespoon ground cinnamon (colorant)

Bay rose: This recipe produces an unexpected spicy rose scent in an off-white soap. Add:

2 ounces bay essential oil

2 ounces rose fragrance oil

Almond and oatmeal complexion bar: I made this off-white, speckled soap in response to a request for a soap that would remove makeup. Add:

4 ounces almond fragrance oil

1 ounce ground almonds

1 ounce ground oatmeal

For superfatting, use 1 1/2 ounces olive oil and 1/2 ounce vitamin E oil.

Aphrodite's spicy love soap: Patchouli's reputation as an aphrodisiac inspired this light brown, speckled soap. Add:

2 ounces patchouli essential oil

1 ounce Peru balsam essential oil

1 ounce clove essential oil

1 tablespoon ground clove (colorant)

Cleopatra's secret: This soap is creamy white with speckles. Add:

1 ounce noninstant milk powder

1 ounce honey

Mix ingredients together with superfatting olive oil in small bowl. Add 1 cup of soap from pot to mixture and blend thoroughly. Add resulting mixture back into soap.

Rosemary refresher: This is a beautiful green soap with the invigorating and clarifying properties of rosemary. Add:

4 ounces rosemary essential oil

2 ounces each dill weed and ground rosemary (colorants)

Beach Breeze *BODY LOTION*

By Mary Ann Hall

Soothe your winter-weary skin with this fresh-scented creamy lotion. It's easy to make luscious body creams at home—especially now, as lots of small companies are cropping up to supply you with high-quality ingredients, wonderful recipes, and sound advice.

To make lotion, you'll need to invest in two pieces of equipment: a scale that can measure to the tenth ounce and an immersion or stick blender (the type used for making milk shakes).

The base of the lotion recipe is oil. I used sweet almond oil and cocoa butter, a combination that works well on normal skin. If you prefer a lighter lotion, you can substitute fractionated coconut oil. For a richer lotion ideal for dry or mature skin, use jojoba or avocado oil. You can also thicken the consistency of a lotion by using only (or more of) a solid oil such as mango, shea, or cocoa butter. Store these versions in wide-mouthed jars or containers since the mixture will be too thick to pour.

Other ingredients include glycerin, a humectant that serves to pull in moisture from the air and keeps your skin more moist; grapefruit seed extract (GSE), a natural preservative; and citric acid, which raises the acidity of lotions, making them less inviting to bacteria. A final ingredient, plant-based emulsifying wax, thickens the lotion. (If you are a label reader like me, you'll see this ingredient in many commercial products.)

To scent your lotion, try an upbeat fragrance. A fashion writer said Petit Cherie smelled like "a day at the beach"—sun, sand, ocean, and suntan lotion. It's a sparkling essence with fruity notes of apple and pear. The heart is a floral bouquet of lily with sensual jasmine, with a drydown of rich musk and precious woods. (See Sweet Cakes in "Resources," pages 78–79.) Or you may scent the lotion with an essential oil such as lavender, rose, geranium, or lime, or a fragrance oil like rose, lilac, or vanilla.

Materials

2.0 ounces sweet almond oil

0.8 ounce glycerin

0.4 ounce cocoa butter

0.4 ounce emulsifying wax

Pinch of citric acid

6.2 ounces distilled water

0.5 ounce grapefruit seed extract (GSE) (5%)

50 drops Petit Cherie or other soap-making scent (optional)

Glass bottles with corks

French Corner labels

Black fine-point marker

Jump rings

Brass charms

Narrow waxed cording or raffia

YOU'LL ALSO NEED:

2-cup Pyrex measuring cup, scale that weighs to 0.1 ounce, microwave oven, spoon, stick blender

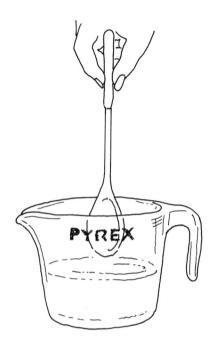

A. Melt first 5 ingredients together in a microwave; stir to dissolve lumps.

Instructions

1. **Make lotion.** Add oil, glycerin, cocoa butter, wax, and citric acid directly to measuring cup, zeroing scale after each addition. Microwave on high for 20 seconds; then stir to dissolve lumps. Repeat until fully liquefied (illustration A). Stir in room-temperature water (mixture will turn milky), GSE, and scent. Immerse blender into cup and blend for 45 seconds.

2. **Package lotion.** Pour lotion into glass bottles. Lotion will thicken slightly as it cools. Insert corks into bottles. Write on label and adhere to center of bottle. Attach jump ring to each charm. Wrap several rows of cording around neck of bottle, inserting jump ring of charm onto

B. Decorate bottle with hand-written label, waxed cording, and a brass charm.

cording (illustration B). Tie off at back of bottle; clip ends. Or wrap a strand of raffia around neck of bottle; knot in front and clip ends.

More Luscious Lotions

FOLLOW THE BASE recipe instructions to blend these exciting variations.

MANGO SPICE

0.4 ounce emulsifying wax

2.4 ounces mango butter

0.8 ounce glycerin

1 gram citric acid

4.8 ounces of distilled water

30 to 60 drops "Mango Spice" synergy (See Rainbow Meadow in "Resources," pages 78–79)

Store this lotion in a jar; it's a bit too thick for a pump or squeeze bottle.

"ALLO" ALOE

0.4 ounce emulsifying wax

2.4 ounces mango butter

0.8 ounce glycerin

1 gram citric acid

4.8 ounces distilled aloe

15 drops peppermint essential oil

15 drops spearmint essential oil

Dispense this creamy lotion from a pump or squeeze bottle.

These recipes were developed by and are the copyright of Melody Upham, owner and founder of Rainbow Meadow, Inc. Martingale & Company would like to thank Ms. Upham, who acted as a consultant.

LIP BALM

By Mary Ann Hall

This recipe allows you to formulate a custom blend. Formulating recipes for your own cosmetics is a creative and earth-friendly alternative to buying commercial products. Lip balms, in particular, are easy and fun to make. After lots of reading, testing, and chatting with enthusiastic experts, I came up with a master lip balm recipe that you can use as a starting point.

Lip balm has two primary components: wax and carrier oil. Essentially, all you do is melt them together in a microwave. From there, you can add or omit optional ingredients to come up with a blend that is perfect for your skin, your senses, and your tastes.

I tested beeswax in three different forms: pearls, granulated, and pastilles. I also tested granulated candelilla wax, which is derived from the candelilla plant found in Mexico and the Southwestern United States. All the forms of these waxes work extremely well and eliminate the added labor of grating or chopping up wax chunks.

I also tested five types of carrier oils: sweet almond oil, avocado oil, hempseed oil, olive oil, and castor oil. The first three were my personal favorites. I found the olive flavor of virgin olive oil too strong and would recommend using a lighter, nonvirgin oil. Castor oil added a nice texture and would be a good choice if you prefer the minty, herbal, medicinal types of lip balms.

Secondary components, such as vitamin E oil, honey, cocoa or shea butter, fragrance oils, and colorants, can be added or omitted as you choose. Cocoa butter and shea butter have natural emulsifying properties, as does vitamin E oil, which is also a preservative. If you want to make a scented lip balm, cocoa butter will add a chocolate note. Many people flavor lip balm with the kind of flavoring oils used in candy and bakery products. I prefer fragrance oils that have been specifically designed for use on the lips, because they are much more subtle. You sense them more than you taste them. The only natural flavoring I recommend is honey, which adds just the slightest hint of sweetness and masks any oily or waxy flavor.

Another option for personalizing your lip balm is to add coloring. The powdered pigments that I used, which are also used to color commercial lipsticks, come with a small 15cc scoop. One 15cc scoop of pigment will add a subtle tint to the pot, but not your lips, while adding additional scoops will eventually create a deeply colored sheer gloss that may tint your lips slightly. In order to get the pigment to dissolve completely, mix it with a little carrier oil first and allow it to set while you mix the rest of the ingredients.

Materials for Lip Balm

MAKES 6 OUNCES OF LIP BALM

Twelve ½-ounce tins

¼ cup plus 2 tablespoons carrier oil

4 tablespoons wax pearls/pastilles OR 2 tablespoons plus 2 teaspoons granulated wax

1 teaspoon honey

½ teaspoon vitamin E oil

½ teaspoon cocoa butter or shea butter (optional)

15cc to 45cc powdered color pigment (optional)

2 to 3 drops fragrance oil (optional)

YOU'LL ALSO NEED:

1-cup Pyrex measuring cup, microwave oven or double boiler, measuring spoons, chopstick (for stirring), teaspoon

Materials for Decorated Tins

MAKES 12 DECORATED TINS

Twelve ½-ounce tins from lip balm project

1.5 ounces ivory Pebeo Porcelaine

Pebeo Porcelaine cloisonné outliner: Vermeil 08, Copper 09

YOU'LL ALSO NEED:

Cotton balls; rubbing alcohol; round, fine-tipped sable brush; cotton rag; cookie sheet; cooling rack

---

Designer's Tip

If you don't have vitamin E oil, you can squeeze the amount needed from vitamin E capsules.

Selecting Your Ingredients

CARRIER OILS

Sweet almond oil: very pale yellow; moisturizing and nourishing for all skin types; rich in protein.

Avocado oil: dark green; heals dry, mature, or dehydrated skin; contains vitamins A, D, E, and protein.

Hempseed oil: greenish gold; obtained from the seeds of a tall Asiatic herb; a balanced moisturizing oil; smooths and softens skin.

Castor oil: colorless to pale yellow; obtained from the beans of a tropical plant; soothing to skin; strong aroma is suitable for minty, herbal, or medicinal balms.

Olive oil: light green to yellow; soothes and moisturizes by penetrating skin with proteins, vitamins, and minerals; for less pronounced flavor, use a light pure olive oil instead of virgin olive oil.

WAXES

Beeswax: a soft substance secreted by honeybees to build honeycombs; ranges in color from off-white to caramel-yellow depending on how much it is filtered; available in three forms for easy measuring: granulated, pearls, and pastilles.

Candelilla wax: a hard vegetable wax derived from the scales of the candelilla plant, which grows in dry, rugged climates; available in granulated form; preferred by vegans.

OTHER INGREDIENTS

Cocoa butter: a vegetable fat extracted from the beans of the tropical cacao tree in the process of making chocolate; softens skin; thickens balms.

Shea butter (also called Karite butter): a thick, white fat extracted from the seeds of an African tree; softens skin.

Vitamin E oil: promotes elasticity and acts as a preservative for other oils.

Flavoring oils: Some of my favorites are creamy vanilla, apricot, blueberry, floriental, natural tangerine, and coconut.

Colorants: FDA-approved cosmetic-grade colorants with names like D&C Red #6 are available in small packets of fine powder with half-pea-size 15cc measuring spoons.

1. **Prepare tins.** Wash tins in warm soapy water and dry thoroughly. Paint tins, if desired (see "Instructions for Decorated Tins," pages 22 and 24).

2. **Combine base ingredients.** Place carrier oil and wax in Pyrex cup (see "Selecting Your Ingredients," page 23). Microwave on high about 2 minutes (or place in double boiler) until wax is melted (see illustration A). Immediately add honey to hot liquid and stir with chopstick to dissolve. Stir in vitamin E oil (illustration B).

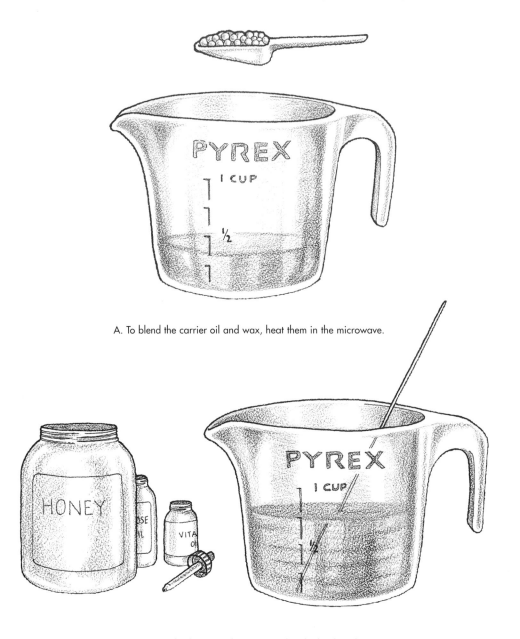

A. To blend the carrier oil and wax, heat them in the microwave.

B. Dissolve honey and vitamin E oil in the hot liquid.

3. **Add optional ingredients.** Add any remaining ingredients one by one, stirring after each addition. To add color, dissolve pigment in a few drops of carrier oil; then add colored oil to balm and stir. Let mixture cool slightly before adding fragrance.

4. **Fill tins.** Dip teaspoon into balm to coat tip. Let balm harden on spoon for a few seconds; apply some to your lips. Adjust as follows until mixture has desired texture: if balm feels too soft or oily, stir in melted wax 1 teaspoon at a time; if too hard or waxy, add more oil in same fashion. Pour balm into individual tins (illustration C). Let cool and harden 20 minutes. Replace lids.

C. Pour the liquid balm into tins and let cool.

Instructions for Decorated Tins

THESE TINS ARE decorated with newly developed, permanent water-based coloring formulas that can be set in an ordinary oven. I have used two products for these easy relief designs—a paint, which I applied with a fine brush, and two cloisonné outliners, which have a thicker consistency than paint and are applied through special pointed tips that come with the tubes.

A. For simple swirls, draw the letter S forward and backward.

B. For snail spirals, draw a small C and keep coiling.

1. **Paint designs on lids.** Clean residual oils and fingerprints from tin lids using cotton ball and alcohol. Apply Pebeo Porcelaine color to top and rim of lids with fine-tipped brush or directly from outliner tube. Use a light touch to make fine designs. Try the following design ideas singly or in combination, using 1 or more colors. Let each color dry 3 minutes before layering over it. Rinse brush in water and dry with rag after each use.

Curled shapes. Paint S-shaped swirls or snail-shaped spirals in a random allover pattern (illustrations A and B). This type of design can stand alone or serve as the background for another design. For a large single spiral, start at the center of the lid and coil outward (illustration C).

Dots. Touch tip of cloisonné outliner to surface, lightly squeeze, and lift up. On lid top, apply dots at random over a swirled background. To space dots evenly around rim, visualize a clock face and fill in the hours (illustration D).

Wedges. Paint 6 or 7 dots around rim; let dry. Paint straight line from one dot toward center; then go back to next dot, forming a V. Repeat all around (illustration E). Fill in wedges with oscillating S curves or other shapes if desired.

2. **Bake on finish.** Let painted lids dry 24 hours in dust-free area. Preheat oven to 300°. Place lids on cookie sheet and bake 35 minutes. Remove from oven, set sheet on rack, and cool 20 minutes or until cool enough to handle. Baked-on finish is permanent and washable.

C. Add a large spiral over a swirled background.

D. Add dots at random or space them around the rim.

E. Use rim dots to plot V-shaped wedges.

Aromatic EGG SOAPS

By Lily Franklin

Appropriately called "melt and pour," these soaps are a breeze to make. These translucent egg soaps require just three supplies: untinted, unscented glycerin soap base; soap-making scent; and liquid food colors (mostly neon). Soap base and soap-making scents can be ordered by mail. The soap is sold in bulk bars for about four dollars per pound, with each pound yielding about five egg soaps. Neon liquid colors are sold in the baking section of craft stores. With the exception of yellow (egg shade), neon colors are essential for producing intense yet clear pastel colors.

I molded these soaps in an egg-shaped plastic Jell-O mold from Kraft Foods (see Jell-O Mold Offer in "Resources," page 78).

To scent your soap, choose a scented oil approved for soap making. Some of the scented oils used for candle making are suitable for soaps as well, but be sure to ask about compatibility, since those that are too harsh can cause the soap to seize. I chose lemon verbena and mint for their fresh, clear, plucky character. These single scents seemed better suited to glycerin soaps than heavy, complex floral scents, which I associate with rich cream soaps.

Materials

MAKES A DOZEN 3-OUNCE SOAPS

2¼ pounds clear glycerin soap
Liquid food colors (see Color-Scent Combinations, page 27)
Scented oil for soap making

YOU'LL ALSO NEED:

1-cup Pyrex measuring cup, plastic wrap, microwave oven, paper coffee cups, plastic spoons, Jell-O 6-compartment egg mold, paring knife

Color-Scent Combinations

Neon green: Minty, grassy, or woodsy scents

Neon pink: Pear, peach, apple, rose

Neon purple: Hyacinth, blueberry

Neon blue: Freesia

Yellow or egg shade: Honeysuckle, citrus, passion flower

Instructions

1. **Melt bulk glycerin.** Cut half of bulk glycerin soap (1⅛ pounds) into small chunks, place in Pyrex cup, and seal with plastic wrap. Microwave on medium for 15 seconds; stir to dissolve chunks. Repeat microwaving in 5-second increments until fully liquefied. Do not overheat or boil or soap will bubble and become cloudy (illustration A).

2. **Add scent and coloring.** Divide liquid soap between 2 paper coffee cups. To each, add 1 drop food color (for neon blue, use ½ drop) and ½ teaspoon scented oil, and stir (illustration B); see chart for suggested

A. Cover soap with plastic wrap and melt in microwave.

B. Add scent and food coloring to soap.

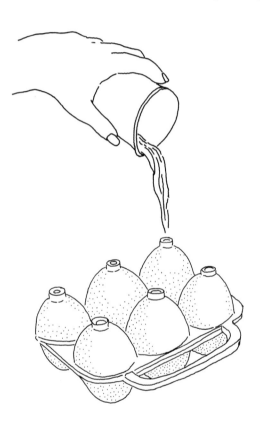

Designer's Tip

To make a split-color egg, fill the mold halfway with one color soap, let set 15 minutes, and then fill to the top with a contrasting color. You can also make striped eggs this way.

color and scent combinations. Be sure to add color conservatively. For better control or to mix colors, squeeze a drop on a spoon, touch another spoon to it, and stir into liquid soap. Repeat to achieve desired tint.

3. **Mold eggs.** Crease coffee-cup rim to make pouring spout. Pour liquid soap into mold, filling 3 egg cavities. Repeat process to pour second cup (illustration C). Let set 30 minutes, and then unmold eggs. Trim off blemishes with paring knife. Wrap each egg individually in piece of 6" x 7" plastic wrap, trimming corners diagonally to reduce bulk. Repeat entire process to melt and mold remaining bulk glycerin.

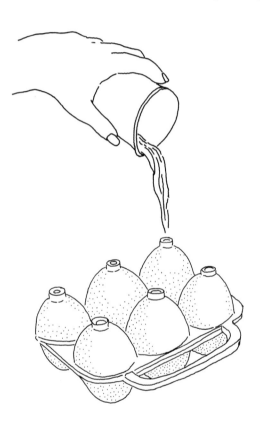

C. Pour soap into mold.

CHAMPAGNE
and CONFETTI LOAF SOAPS

By Kaila Westerman

*M*ake champagne-scented, sliceable soaps for a bubbly New Year's gift. These fanciful confetti soaps are made in two steps. First you layer colored soaps and slice them into sticks. Next, place the sticks into a tube mold (or length of PVC pipe) as you would swizzle sticks in a glass and add more soap. When the soap hardens, slice it into palm-sized bars, revealing the pattern.

Materials

1 pound clear or white glycerin melt-and-pour soap
3 or 4 cosmetic-grade colorants
8" tube mold or length of PVC pipe
¼ ounce cosmetic-grade glitter or sparkle powder
Champagne-scented fragrance oil for soap making

YOU'LL ALSO NEED:

Aluminum foil, 1-cup Pyrex measuring cup, plastic wrap, microwave oven, measuring teaspoon, stir sticks, spray bottle, alcohol, knife, plastic tray or container, freezer, glass cutting board, lint-free cloth

---

Designer's Tip

To vary this recipe, try coordinating the soap color with the fragrance. Below are some suggestions to choose from. For best results, scent your soap with a single scent or pick a theme (such as floral or fruit) and use a combination of two or three fragrance oils related to that theme.

COLOR	SCENT IDEAS
Yellow	Banana, perfect pineapple
Blue	Ocean rain, blueberry
Pink	Rose, grapefruit
Orange	Orange blossom, tropical squeeze
Green	Crisp cucumber, meadow breeze, northwoods

Instructions

1. **Make soap swizzle sticks.** Shape foil into a 4" x 6" x ½" rectangular tray. Cut 2 oz. of soap (⅛ of soap block) into chunks. Place chunks into Pyrex cup and cover with plastic wrap. Microwave on medium until liquefied (illustration A).

A. Cover soap with plastic wrap and melt in microwave.

Do not overheat or boil soap. Stir in 1 teaspoon of colorant and pour into foil tray (illustration B).

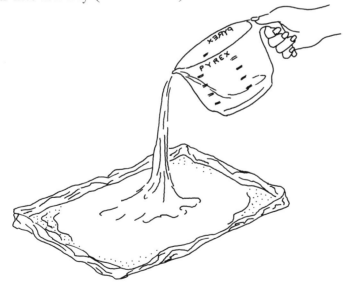

B. Layer colored soaps in foil tray.

When surface is firm but still warm, spritz with alcohol. Repeat to add 2 more colored layers, letting cool slightly before you pour. Let layers firm up; then peel off foil, slice soap into ⅛"-thick sticks, twist each stick, place on plastic tray or in plastic container, and store in freezer (illustration C).

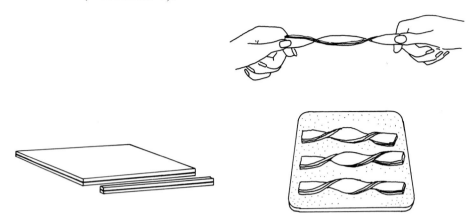

C. Twist soap sticks and store in freezer.

2. **Add glitter and scent to soap.** Melt a small amount of soap, pour it onto a glass cutting board, and stand the tube mold upright in it to seal the bottom end. Melt the remaining soap, let cool until no longer steaming, and then stir in glitter or sparkle powder and a few drops of fragrance oil.

3. **Mold soap.** Stand the frozen swizzle sticks randomly in the mold. Pour in cooled sparkle soap (no steam rising and a visible skin on top) and let it harden overnight (illustration D).

D. Pour sparkle soap into mold over frozen soap sticks.

4. **Slice soap.** Soak mold in warm water bath for 1 minute, gently push out soap, and wipe down with clean, lint-free cloth. Slice soap into 1" bars.

Polka Dot SOAP DISH *and* TUMBLER

By Genevieve A. Sterbenz

Ceramic paints liven up any plain ceramic soap dish and tumbler and ensure that they will match your bathroom decor perfectly.

Here, dots of fuchsia pink and saffron are applied to a soap dish and tumbler set in a random pattern to create a modern and colorful look that is very simple to do.

Ceramic paints are available in a wide variety of colors and can be applied very easily. Depending on your skill level, you can create a simple dot pattern like the one shown here, add "his" and "hers" to matching tumblers, or craft something more detailed, like a floral pattern or decorative border. I found that it was best to apply the paint with cotton swabs instead of a paintbrush because swabs don't leave brush strokes in a thick coat of paint. (Thick coats create a greater saturation of color.) Paintbrushes do work very well for small details and one-coat applications.

The ceramic paints I chose are water-soluble, which makes cleanup easy and allows for corrections. This paint requires heat setting in a regular household oven for thirty-five minutes in order for the design to become permanent. So if you make a mistake or change your mind while working, you can wash away the pattern with soap and water, as long as you have not yet set it by baking.

Materials

MAKES 1 SOAP DISH AND 1 TUMBLER

Ceramic soap dish and tumbler in white
Ceramic paint in fuchsia and saffron (Pebeo Porcelaine 150 Ceramic Paints)

YOU'LL ALSO NEED:

Dish soap, paper towels, cotton swabs, baking pan, aluminum foil, oven

1. **Prepare and paint soap dish and tumbler.** Thoroughly wash and dry soap dish and tumbler to remove all grease, dust, and dirt. Set soap dish aside. Dip a cotton swab into fuchsia paint and create 1 vertical column of dots on the tumbler. Create a second vertical column of dots to the right of the first, shifting placement of the dots so each dot falls between 2 dots in the previous column (illustration A). Since my tumbler tapered slightly toward the bottom, I placed my columns about 1¼" apart near the top and tapered them slightly at the bottom so the columns were about 1" apart. Continue adding columns of dots in this fashion over surface area of tumbler. Let dry.

   Using a clean cotton swab, dip into saffron paint and create circles around outside edge of fuchsia dots (illustration B).

   Following manufacturer's directions, let dry for 24 hours. Repeat painting process for the soap dish, painting the top, underside, and stem of the dish.

2. **Set paint.** Following manufacturer's directions, place soap dish and tumbler on baking pan covered with aluminum foil and place in preheated oven set to 300°F for 35 minutes. Let cool.

A. Paint dots on tumbler with a cotton swab.

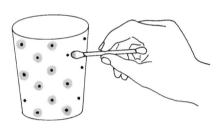

B. Paint circles around each dot with a cotton swab.

Designer's Tip

After a few applications of paint, your cotton swab may begin to lose its round shape or to have stray "threads." Be sure to replace cotton swabs regularly to maintain proper application of paint.

Daisy SHOWER CURTAIN

By Dawn Anderson

Restyle your bathroom in an afternoon with a fresh-looking gingham shower curtain accented with daisy appliqués. Hang the curtain with polka dot rings for a custom finish.

You can achieve this look with an ordinary bed sheet, some daisy appliqué trim, and a small amount of yellow craft paint. To make the curtain, simply trim a full-size sheet to size, hem the four sides, and install grommets along the top. I clipped the daisies from appliqué trim that comes by the yard. Two sizes were used for this project: 1" and 1½" daisies. A yard of daisies costs around five dollars—much less than the cost of individual appliqués. Because one of my appliqué trims was solid white, I colored the daisy centers with yellow craft paint. Once they dried, I adhered the daisies to the shower curtain with liquid fusible web. This adhesive bonds well and withstands laundering.

To complete the curtain, I painted the plastic shower curtain rings with yellow dots to echo the daisy appliqués. I prepped the surface of the rings and used a durable paint, followed by a gloss finish for permanence.

Materials

MAKES 1 SHOWER CURTAIN AND 12 SHOWER CURTAIN RINGS

Full-size bed sheet
Thread to match sheet
Twelve ⁵⁄₁₆" grommets and grommet setter and anvil
2½ yards daisy appliqué trim, with daisies about 1" in diameter
1 yard daisy appliqué trim, with daisies about 1½" in diameter
Liqui-fuse liquid fusible web
Twelve shower curtain rings
Delta CeramDecor Perm Enamel Surface Cleaner and Conditioner
Delta CeramDecor Perm Enamel in citrus yellow
Delta CeramDecor Perm Enamel Clear Gloss Glaze

YOU'LL ALSO NEED:

Self-healing cutting mat; rotary cutter; sewing shears; iron and ironing board; sewing machine; clear acrylic grid ruler; chalk pencil; ¼" hole punch; hammer; pins; 2 press cloths; #0000 steel wool; paper towels; cotton swabs; paint palette or plastic lid; ⅛"-wide, flat paintbrush

SHOWER CURTAIN

1. **Sew shower curtain. Cut a 76"-wide x 76½"-long rectangle from full-size sheet.** Press up and stitch a 1" double-fold hem along the lower edge; repeat along the sides. Press up and stitch a 1¼" double-fold hem along the upper edge.

2. **Install grommets.** Mark spacing of grommets along upper edge of shower curtain with chalk pencil; space end grommets 1½" from sides of curtain, centered on hem allowance. Space remaining grommets evenly between end grommets, about 6¼" apart (illustration A).

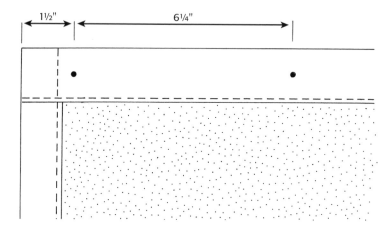

A. Mark grommet placement across the top of shower curtain.

Punch holes at marked points. Insert front of grommet through hole in fabric from front side; rest grommet on anvil. Position grommet back in place. Place grommet setter over extended portion of grommet front and hammer until grommet is securely fastened in place (illustration B).

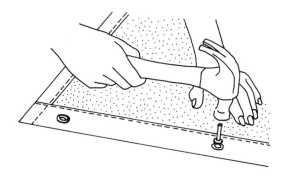

B. Install grommets with setting tool and hammer.

3. **Attach daisy appliqués.** Clip daisy appliqués apart. Mark placement of appliqués on shower curtain with pins. Space rows of daisies 7" apart with daisies 9" apart within each row. Start odd-numbered rows 4½" from the side edges and start even-numbered rows 9" from the side edges (illustration C).

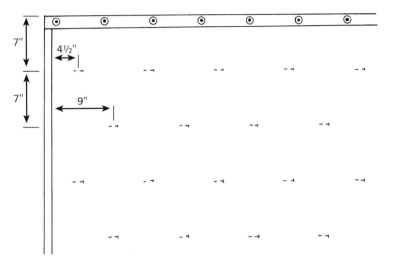

C. Mark placement of appliqués.

The last row will be positioned 2" from the lower edge of the curtain.

Cover ironing board with press cloth. Plan arrangement of daisies at pin marks (I alternated the placement of small and large daisies, creating a pattern that repeated across the sheet). Place dot of Liquifuse at center of wrong side of daisy; press in place on shower curtain; cover with press cloth. Press with iron 40–50 seconds. Turn curtain over and press from wrong side to be sure daisy is fused in place. Repeat for remaining daisies.

SHOWER CURTAIN RINGS

Paint shower curtain rings. Degloss plastic rings by rubbing with steel wool; rinse, and then dry. Apply Perm Enamel Surface Cleaner and Conditioner to rings, following manufacturer's recommendations. Paint dots on rings with cotton swab; space dots about ½" apart; allow to dry 1 hour (illustration D).

Apply 2 coats of Perm Enamel Clear Gloss Glaze to shower curtain rings, allowing to dry 1 hour between coats. Allow to dry 10 days.

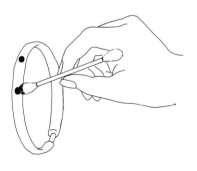

D. Paint dots on shower curtain rings using a cotton swab.

ENVELOPE SLIPCOVER
for a BATH PILLOW

By Genevieve A. Sterbenz

Enhance the experience of relaxing in your home bath with elegant sup-
port for your head. Using organza and rayon fabric in refreshing citrus colors and
a simple envelope pattern, you can create a romantic slipcover that conceals the
most ordinary of vinyl bath pillows. The envelope shape allows the slipcover to be
removed easily so that it can be washed or dried. Buttonholes stitched on the back
of the slipcover allow the four small suction cups of the vinyl pillow to attach to the
tub at the desired location.

When choosing fabric for the cover of your bath pillow, pick light-weight fabrics. Synthetic ones work very well because they will dry in a short time, avoiding the dampness associated with thicker fabrics. Be sure not to use fabrics with metallic fibers, as these may rust.

I chose a soft floral trim that would not be uncomfortable when used to accent the front of the slipcover. It is cotton and won't be a problem when it gets wet. Keep this in mind when choosing a trim for your own slipcover. Polyester trims will also work nicely, as they are washable. The beads added at the base of the slipcover give the flap some weight to keep it closed. And because the beads hang so low, they will not interfere with the comfort of the pillow.

Materials

MAKES 1 SLIPCOVER FOR A BATH PILLOW

Vinyl bath pillow with suction cups, 11" x 7" x 1½"

⅞ yard iridescent lime green organza

⅞ yard apple green rayon lining fabric

1½ yards variegated ribbon rose trim in apricot (Mokuba)

3 green 2 mm beads

2 gold 4 mm beads

1 green 15 mm bead

1 clear 10 mm bead

Thread to match fabrics

Use of photocopy machine, scissors, iron and ironing board, sewing shears, pins, sewing machine, hand-sewing needle, dressmaker's tracing paper, dull pencil, clear acrylic grid ruler

Instructions

1. **Prepare pattern and cut fabric.** Photocopy patterns (page 44) for envelope slipcover and buttonhole facing, enlarging buttonhole facing pattern 125% and slipcover pattern 320%. Cut out patterns along outer marked lines. Press fabrics. Cut 1 slipcover piece and 4 buttonhole facing pieces, each from organza and lining.

2. **Sew organza and lining together.** Lay organza on protected work surface. Position lining fabric over organza, right sides together; pin. Stitch ½" from all edges, removing pins as you come to them. Leave 4"-long opening between dots for turning. Trim seam allowances to ¼". Clip curves and trim corners; then turn slipcover to right side. Slipstitch opening closed. Press, using iron on appropriate setting for fabric type; set aside.

3. **Prepare buttonhole facings.** Layer each of 4 squares of organza fabric over 4 squares of lining fabric, right sides up, matching raw edges. Zigzag layers together around all sides for each set of layered squares; set aside.

4. **Make buttonholes.** Lay slipcover, organza side up, on flat surface. Reposition pattern on slipcover. Use straight pins to mark position of buttonholes. Remove pattern carefully, keeping pins in place. Place dressmaker's tracing paper over buttonhole facing pieces. Position facing pattern on top, aligning edges of pattern with edges of fabric. Transfer buttonhole markings by tracing over pattern lines with a dull pencil. Mark both stitching and cutting lines (illustration A).

Pin buttonhole facing pieces on slipcover, organza sides together, aligning short ends of buttonhole markings on facings with pin marks on slipcover. Machine-stitch on dashed stitching lines. Using scissors, cut slit through center of buttonholes and to corners, following marked solid cutting lines. Turn all 4 facings to wrong side of slipcover; press.

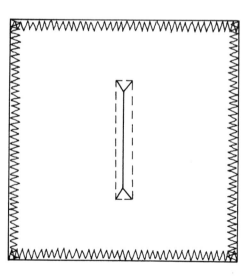

A. Mark buttonhole placement on each facing piece.

5 **Sew slipcover.** Lay slipcover, organza side up, on flat surface. Fold up bottom third on foldline, using pattern as a guide; pin sides. Machine-stitch sides ¼" from edges. To accommodate thickness of pillow, flatten seam at corner, aligning side seam with bottom foldline and sew across corner, about ¾" in from corner (illustration B).

Repeat at opposite corner; turn slipcover to right side.

6 **Add trim.** Align trim along outer edge of slipcover flap; pin, trimming excess and turning under ¼" at ends. Handstitch in place, stitching through top layer of organza fabric only. Repeat to stitch a second row of trim inside the first row, spacing stitching lines of trim ¾" apart. Taper second row to meet first row at ends (illustration C).

7 **Add beads.** Using threaded hand-sewing needle, stitch two 2 mm green beads to center of flap ⅜" above trim and ⅜" apart. Stitch the third 2 mm bead to center of flap just above outer row of trim. Tie knot and trim excess thread. Take a small stitch at point of flap to secure thread. String beads in the following order: one 4 mm gold, one 15 mm green, one 10 mm clear, and one 4 mm gold. Insert needle back through first 3 beads to starting point. Take a stitch and repeat to secure beads in place, making a beaded "tassel" (illustration D).

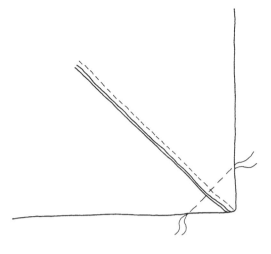

B. Sew across corner to give depth to slipcover.

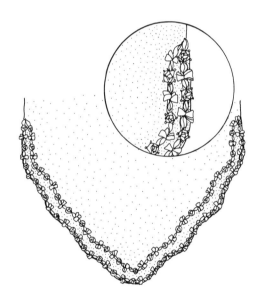

C. Stitch 2 rows of trim to flap of slipcover.

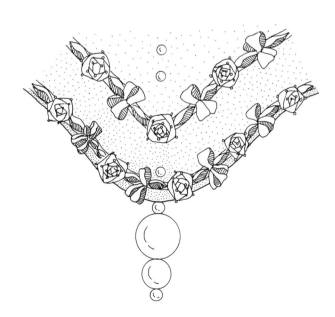

D. Sew beads to flap of slipcover.

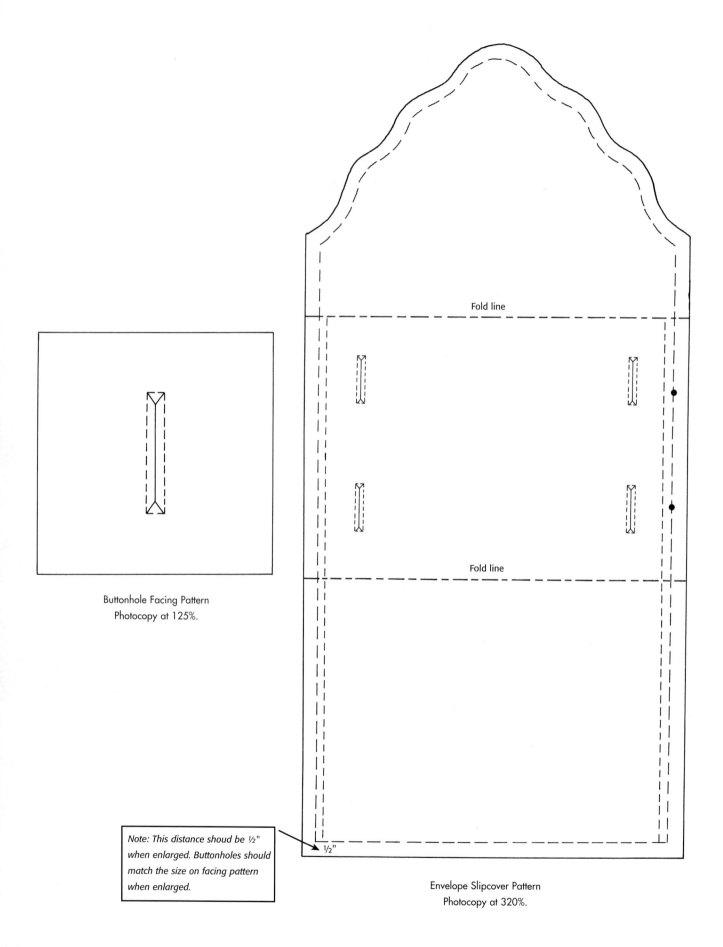

Buttonhole Facing Pattern
Photocopy at 125%.

Note: This distance shoud be ½"
when enlarged. Buttonholes should
match the size on facing pattern
when enlarged.

Fold line

Fold line

½"

Envelope Slipcover Pattern
Photocopy at 320%.

Painted MINI-CHEST

By Dawn Anderson

Keep your bathroom organized by storing items like hair barrettes, rubber bands, ribbons, cosmetics, or jewelry in the drawers of this retro-look mini-chest. For the color-blocked effect shown, you need four paint colors of the same intensity. I mixed my own paints to achieve the colors shown here. If you are mixing paints, be sure to store the paint in a plastic container or cover it with plastic wrap between steps to prevent it from drying out. I used the same paint colors to stamp flower and leaf images onto some of the chest drawers.

To carry the floral theme throughout the project, I glued plastic flower buttons to the front of the drawer pulls. For best results when customizing drawer pulls, use wood knobs that have a diameter smaller than the buttons you are using. You can also substitute ready-made novelty drawer pulls. To customize the chest to your own bathroom décor, simply choose stamp images and drawer pulls in a related theme.

Materials

MAKES 1 CHEST

Wood chest

Wood sealer

6 wood knobs, ¾" in diameter with screws

Acrylic paints in the following colors:

- lavender
- white
- green
- dark goldenrod
- primary yellow
- lemon yellow

2 or 3 rubber stamps

Clear acrylic finish

6 decorative plastic buttons, about 1⅛" in diameter

You'll also need:

Wood filler; pencil; metal ruler; drill and drill bit; 60-grit, 100-grit, and 220-grit sandpaper; spray mister; paper towels; foam brushes; masking tape; ³⁄₈" flat brush; 1 sheet ¹⁄₈" thick craft foam; wire cutter; 5-minute epoxy; liner paint brush (optional); screwdriver

Instructions

1. Prepare chest and knobs. Fill any imperfections in wood with wood filler; allow to dry. Find center of drawer front by drawing diagonal lines between opposite corners of drawer front. Drill hole for knob at intersection of marked lines; repeat for remaining drawers (illustration A).

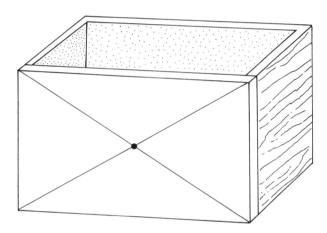

A. Drill hole in center of each drawer at the intersection of marked lines.

Sand chest lightly with 100-grit sandpaper. Remove sanding dust with a lightly misted paper towel. Seal wood with wood sealer. Sand tops of wood knobs flat by rubbing them top down across 60-grit sandpaper.

2. Paint base coat. Mix 1 part green paint, 1 part primary yellow paint, and 1 part white paint to make lime paint; use foam brush to paint top, bottom, and sides of chest, plus 1 drawer front and 1 wood knob with 1 coat of lime paint. Paint 2 drawer fronts and 2 wood knobs with a mixture of 1 part lavender paint and 1 part white paint. Paint 2 drawer fronts and 2 knobs with a mixture of 1 part dark goldenrod paint, 1 part lemon yellow paint, and 2 parts white paint. Paint 1 drawer front and 1 knob with a mixture of 1 part primary yellow paint and 2 parts white paint. Use flat brush to paint chest front with white paint.

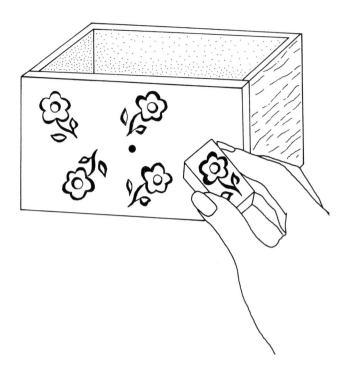

B. Stamp images onto 3 drawer fronts.

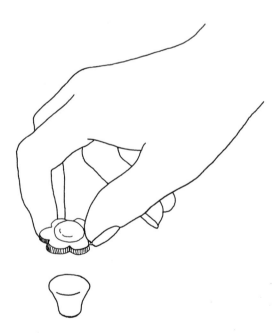

C. Glue flower buttons to tops of wood knobs.

3. **Apply additional coats of paint.** Paint chest, drawers, and knobs with second coat of paint as before; allow to dry. Sand chest, drawers, and knobs lightly with 220-grit sandpaper; remove sanding dust with lightly misted paper towel. Apply a third coat of paint as before.

4. **Stamp drawers.** Place a small pool of paint on craft foam. Brush out paint in both directions to make a smooth, thin, even layer of paint over foam. Tap rubber stamp lightly onto foam a couple times to lightly coat with paint. Press stamp onto drawer front to make impression. Repeat to make 5 to 7 impressions over drawer front, allowing stamp to run off edge of drawer, if necessary (illustration B).

Repeat to stamp 2 additional drawer fronts.

5. **Apply sealer.** Apply clear finish to cabinet, drawer fronts, and knobs, following manufacturer's recommendations.

6. **Prepare and attach knobs.** Trim shanks from back of buttons with a wire cutter. If necessary, glue flower center to flower petal portion of button with 5-minute epoxy, following the manufacturer's recommendations. Allow to dry. Glue flower to top of painted wood knob, following manufacturer's recommendations (illustration C).

Allow to dry for 24 hours. Attach knobs to cabinet.

Embellished HAND TOWELS

By Genevieve A. Sterbenz

Turn plain terry cloth hand towels into whimsical accents for your bathroom. Playful butterfly appliqués in tangerine dance across a field of soft yellow plush terry and are accented with ribbon trims and sweet tiny buttons. Applying the trims to the towels is simple to do. Just be sure to choose trims that are washable, such as ones made from cotton or polyester. The butterfly appliqués may look slightly complicated to apply, but because they are backed with an adhesive, as many appliqué trims are, they can be fused in place by using the heat from an iron to activate the glue. Look for this feature when selecting appliqués.

Although I chose to use a number of different trims, your towels can be as simple or elaborate as you like. It all depends upon your personal style, décor and the intended use. And before you go out and buy all new towels, keep in mind that this can be a great recycling project. If you love the towels you already have, but they are just a bit plain, this is a perfect way to give them and your entire bathroom a whole new look.

Materials

MAKES 2 EMBELLISHED HAND TOWELS

2 terry cloth hand towels in pale yellow, 30" x 18"

1 1/8 yards 1/4"-wide tangerine checked ribbon

1 1/8 yards 1/4"-wide tangerine grosgrain ribbon

1 1/8 yards 1 1/2"-wide tangerine butterfly appliqué trim

1 1/8 yards 1/2"-diameter yellow pompon fringe

Fabric glue

Thread to match trims

14 yellow buttons, 1 cm wide

YOU'LL ALSO NEED:

Scissors, sewing machine, clear acrylic grid ruler, straight pins, iron and ironing board, hand-sewing needle

Designer's Tip

If machine stitching through the thickness of the grosgrain ribbon, pompon fringe, and towel poses a problem for your machine or causes the ribbon to shift, the grosgrain ribbon can be tacked in place with fabric glue and then hand-stitched in place with matching thread and a needle.

Instructions (for 1 towel)

1. **Position and adhere ribbon and pompon fringe trims.** Place 1 towel in vertical position on clean, flat work surface. Measure across 1 short edge of towel and cut 2 lengths each from both ribbons, butterfly appliqué trim, and pompon fringe to the measured length plus an additional ½" for the ribbons and fringe. Set all but 1 length of checked ribbon aside. If towel has a decorative woven band a few inches above each short edge, then center checked ribbon over decorative band at one end of towel, with ends of ribbon extending ¼" beyond towel edges at sides. Secure in place with dabs of glue on wrong side of ribbon, turning in ¼" at each end of ribbon. Allow to dry. If towel does not have a decorative woven band, then secure ribbon to towel 3½" in from one short edge. Repeat process to apply pompon fringe to front towel edge on same side of towel, allowing only pompons and not fringe heading to fall evenly below lower edge of towel. Repeat again to apply grosgrain ribbon to edge of towel along lower edge of pompon fringe heading, flush with lower edge of towel. Edgestitch along all edges of both ribbons, backstitching at ends. Edgestitch along upper edge of pompon fringe, backstitching at ends (illustration A).

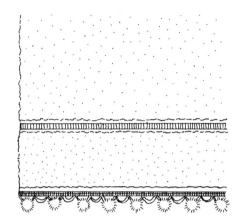

A. Stitch ribbons and pompon fringe in place.

2. **Position and adhere appliqué trim.** Center butterfly appliqué trim on towel between the 2 rows of ribbons; secure with straight pins. Press down iron over trim to activate adhesive, removing pins as you work (illustration B).

    Let cool. Secure in place with small stitches using hand-sewing needle and thread.

3. **Add buttons.** Pin-mark button placement on checked ribbon, spacing at 2" intervals and starting and ending 2" from side edges of towel. Sew buttons in place at pin marks.

B. Press butterfly appliqué trim in place between rows of ribbon and fringe.

Padded SCENTED HANGER

By Dawn Anderson

*P*added hangers add a distinctive yet practical touch to any closet. In addition to bringing elegance to your wardrobe, they keep delicate garments from puckering at the shoulders when they are hung.

This classically designed padded hanger is so easy to assemble that you may want to make a set of three at once. All you need for each one is a wooden dress hanger, fabric, and matching ribbon, cotton batting for the stuffing, and an herbal scented mixture. After cutting fabric pieces from a pattern that you make yourself, prepare scented strips of batting to pad the hanger. To assemble the pieces, you just glue and sew. For a creative touch, hang two scented strawberries from the hook.

I filled my hanger with an herbal moth repellent (including cedar chips, rosemary, southernwood, lavender, and cardamom seed), but you can substitute dried lavender or use a tiny drop of essential oil to scent yours.

Materials

MAKES 1 PADDED HANGER

Wooden dress hanger with screw-in hook

½ yard 45"-wide checked fabric

¼ yard 45"-wide fleece

⅛ yard 45"-wide pindot fabric

12" x 45" piece of cotton batting

2 cups mixed herbal ingredients

1¼ yards ¼"-wide variegated green ribbon (Mokuba)

White craft glue

Double-sided tape

Sewing thread to match fabrics

Upholstery thread

Six 1"-long velvet leaves

YOU'LL ALSO NEED:

Strawberry pattern (see page 58), tracing paper, ruler, pins, pencil, scissors, hand-sewing needle, iron and ironing board, sewing machine, sewing shears

1. **Prepare patterns.** Photocopy strawberry pattern (see page 58), enlarging 125%. To make custom hanger pattern, lay wooden hanger flat on tracing paper and trace around wooden portion with pencil. Draft new line 1" beyond traced line, rounding off corners slightly (illustration A).

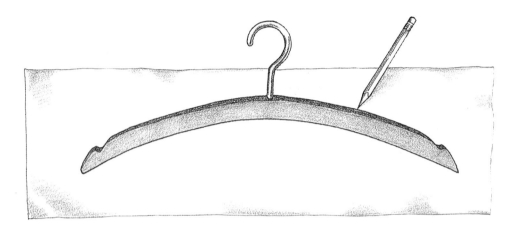

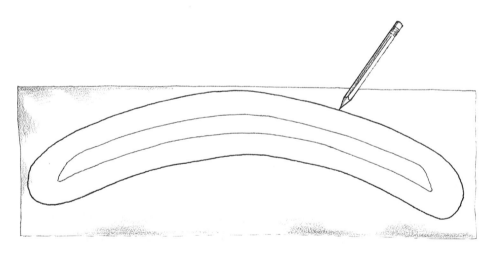

A. For a custom pattern, trace your hanger's outline and add a 1" allowance all around.

2. **Cut fabric and batting.** Fold checked fabric on bias. Place hanger pattern parallel to folded edge and pin (illustration B). Using shears, cut along pattern outline through both layers. Also cut 2 hanger pieces from fleece for the lining. Using strawberry pattern, cut 4 strawberries from pindot fabric and 4 from batting.

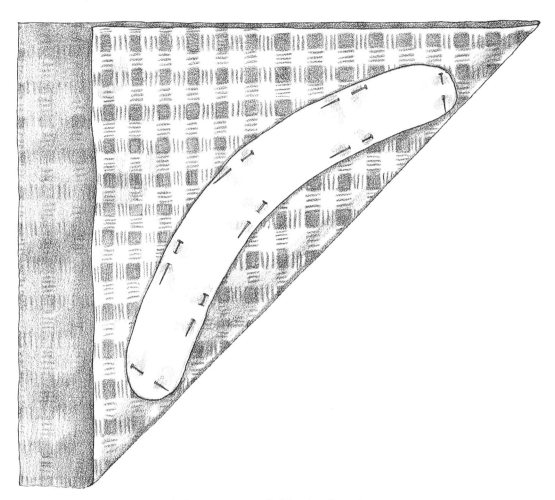

B. Place the hanger pattern on the fabric bias for cutting.

3. **Prepare scented batting strips.** Cut three 3" x 45" strips from batting. Split 1 strip into 2 plies by separating and peeling back the top layer. Sift through herbal mixture with your fingers and discard any large or hard ingredients. Sprinkle half onto bottom ply of batting; replace top layer to cover it (illustration C). Repeat process to layer remaining mixture inside second batting strip. Leave third strip as it is.

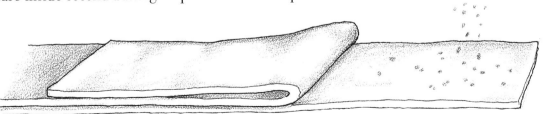

C. Sprinkle herbal scented mixture between plies of batting.

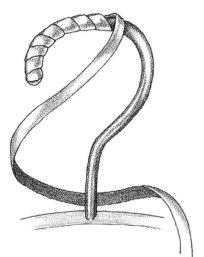

D. Wrap narrow ribbon around the hanger hook, gluing as you go.

COVERING THE HANGER

1. **Glue ribbon to hanger hook.** Cut 12" length from ribbon and set it aside. Apply glue to tip of hook. Fold end of remaining ribbon yardage over tip, and then wrap ribbon around tip, concealing ribbon end. Apply glue to next ½" section of hook and wrap ribbon around it. Continue gluing and wrapping in ½" intervals (illustration D). When you reach wooden portion of hanger, trim ribbon ½" beyond hook and glue down.

2. **Pad hanger.** Affix double-sided tape to front and back of wooden hanger. Starting at one end, wind 1 scented batting strip around hanger in a spiral wrap. When you reach middle of hanger, clip strip to accommodate hook and continue spiraling, adding second scented strip as necessary (illustration E). When you reach end, trim off and save excess strip. Finish padding hanger by wrapping plain strip around it.

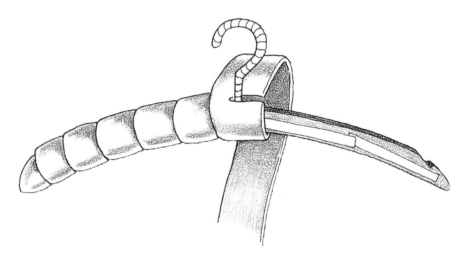

E. Pad the hanger with the scented batting.

3. **Sew hanger cover.** Lay 1 fleece hanger piece flat. Place checked hanger piece on top, right side up. Baste ¼" from raw edges all around through both layers. Repeat process to layer and baste second fleece-checked hanger pair. Place both pairs fabric sides together and pin. Beginning at one end, machine-stitch curved ends and long underside curve ¼" from edges (illustration F). Clip curves; turn right side out.

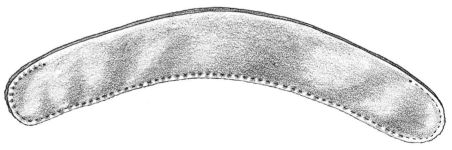

F. To make the cover, sew 2 fleece-lined pieces together.

4. **Fit cover on hanger.** Stuff small wad of excess batting into each curved end of cover until firm. Insert hanger into cover through open top; fit should be snug but not tight. To increase padding, cut new 3" x 45" strip from batting, separate plies, and wrap one more ply around hanger, as in previous step. To decrease padding, remove final batting strip, separate plies, and rewrap hanger with 1 ply only. To finish upper seam, fold one edge under ¼", lap it over other edge, and slipstitch closed; make firm stitches at base of hook (illustration G). Steam-press seams.

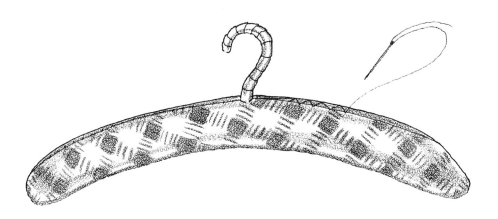

G. Turn the cover right side out, fit the hanger inside, and stitch the open edge closed.

MAKING THE STRAWBERRIES

1. **Sew strawberries.** Lay 1 batting strawberry flat. Place pindot strawberry on top, right side up, and baste ¼" from raw edges all around. Repeat process for 4 strawberry shapes (2 for each strawberry). Pin 2 strawberries fabric sides together and machine stitch between dots (illustration H). Clip curves; turn right side out. Repeat process for remaining pair of strawberries.

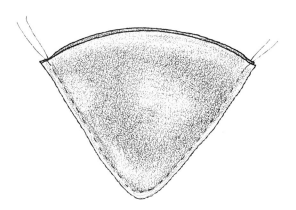

H. Sew 2 fleece-lined strawberry pieces together to make a pocket.

2. **Stuff strawberries.** Place one end of 12" ribbon even with top edge of strawberry and machine tack in place. Using upholstery thread, hand sew gathering stitches ¼" from upper edge all around (illustration I). Stuff strawberry with leftover scented batting; pull thread ends to cinch opening as tightly as possible. Using eraser end of pencil, push additional batting into cavity until strawberry is firm. Stitch securely, retacking ribbon if necessary (illustration J). Join second strawberry to opposite end of ribbon, gather edge by hand, and stuff it in same way.

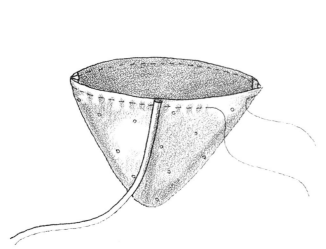

I. Turn the pocket, tack on ribbon, and hand-gather the edge.

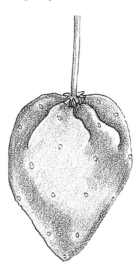

J. Stuff the strawberry and gather the edge closed.

3. **Glue leaves to strawberries.** Using scissors, trim stem end of 6 leaves at a 60° angle. Using white craft glue, affix 3 leaves to top of each strawberry, butting angled edges (illustration K). Allow outer edges near leaf tips to curl up for a natural look. To join strawberries to hanger, wind ribbon a few times around base of hook.

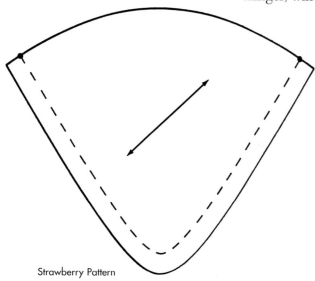

Strawberry Pattern
Photocopy at 125%.

K. Glue velvet leaves to the top to conceal the puckering.

Blown Glass BOTTLE STOPPERS

By Dawn Anderson

For bottles with short necks, you can shorten the cork by sawing off the lower half with a small handsaw and sanding the bottom of the cork smooth with fine sandpaper.

Create this collection of bottle stoppers from exquisite blown glass beads in just a few hours. Use these decorative bottles for storing bath salts. Create several to give as gifts.

The hollow glass beads, made in Venice, are available by mail (see Beads and Beyond in "Resources," page 78). Look for decorative glass bottles at craft stores or stores carrying kitchen or garden items. For each bottle, choose a hollow blown glass bead that goes with it in size and color. You'll also need a small glass accent bead, a small bead cap, a 3"-long unadorned hat pin, and a brass knob escutcheon (found at stores carrying cabinet hardware). Choose a round escutcheon that covers the top of the cork. If your bottle doesn't come with a cork, you can find corks in a variety of sizes at hardware stores.

Materials

MAKES 1 BOTTLE STOPPER

Glass bottle

Cork that fits bottle opening

Hat pin at least 3" long

Brass escutcheon with diameter about the same as top of cork

Small accent bead

One 5 mm bead cap

Hollow glass Venetian bead, about 1" in diameter

YOU'LL ALSO NEED:

E6000 glue, wire cutters, needle file

Instructions

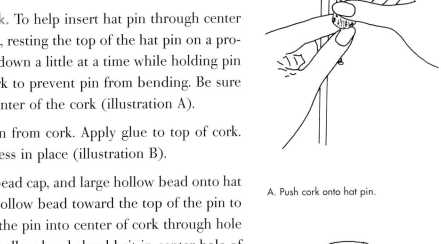

A. Push cork onto hat pin.

1. **Push hat pin into center of cork.** To help insert hat pin through center of cork, turn cork upside down, resting the top of the hat pin on a protected work surface; pull cork down a little at a time while holding pin between fingers just under cork to prevent pin from bending. Be sure pin exits at the approximate center of the cork (illustration A).

2. **Attach escutcheon.** Remove pin from cork. Apply glue to top of cork. Center escutcheon on cork; press in place (illustration B).

3. **Add beads.** Place small bead, bead cap, and large hollow bead onto hat pin; position smallest hole in hollow bead toward the top of the pin to be covered by bead cap. Push the pin into center of cork through hole as far as it will go; bottom of hollow bead should sit in center hole of escutcheon (illustration C). Allow glue to dry.

B. Glue escutcheon to top of cork.

C. Thread beads, bead cap, and cork onto hat pin.

4. **Trim hat pin.** Use wire cutters to trim hat pin even with bottom of cork. File off bottom of pin until even with bottom of cork.

Drawer-Liner SACHETS

By Elizabeth Cameron

There is something indescribably luxurious about being greeted by the scent of lavender or freesia every time you open a drawer. These sachets are essentially rice paper envelopes of potpourri that lie flat along the bottom of your drawer.

Take your drawer measurements along when you go to the art supply store to select your sheets of rice paper. Choose lightweight rice papers that will allow the scent to circulate; you will need to buy two sheets for each drawer. Cut the rice paper with a rotary cutter or sewing shears as you would a fabric. The fibers that make up rice paper are longer and tougher than those in wood pulp papers, so using a craft knife may result in a tear rather than a clean cut. Once paper is cut to size, glue two sheets together on three edges to create a pouch; then fill it with any combination of dried flowers or potpourri.

It's not necessary to decorate your sachet, since the shapes of the petals and leaves will show through the diaphanous papers and can be quite pretty on their own, but I decided to add gold accents to dress up the sachets for gift giving. To create corner accents I used fan-shaped jewelry findings snipped in half to yield quarter-circles. I also added a monogram with gold letters. Small triangles of Velcro on the underside of each corner hold the sachet secure at the bottom of the drawer.

Materials

MAKES 1 CUSTOM-SIZE LINER

1 to 2 sheets rice paper
Yes Stikflat glue
1" to 2" gold foil letters (for monogram)
Two 1 ½" gold filigree fans
Dried flowers or herbs (e.g., rose petals, freesia, lavender)
1" x 2" strip white self-adhesive Velcro

YOU'LL ALSO NEED:

Tape measure; rotary cutter; clear acrylic grid ruler; self-healing cutting mat; flat, stiff 1" brush; tin snips; scissors

1. **Make rice paper envelope.** Measure inside drawer bottom, e.g., 15" x 30". Using rotary cutter, grid ruler, and mat, cut 2 rectangles of rice paper ⅛" larger than bottom of drawer. Brush ½" strip of glue around 3 edges of 1 sheet. Place second sheet on top, align edges, and press to adhere (illustration A). Let dry 10 minutes. Use cutting tools to trim uneven edges and to square corners. Test-fit in drawer; retrim if necessary.

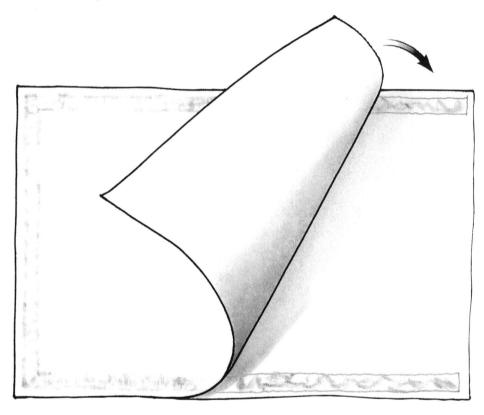

A. Glue 2 pieces of rice paper together on 3 sides.

2. **Decorate sleeve.** Center monogram letters on pouch front, glue, and press to adhere. Using tin snips, cut each gold filigree fan in half to yield 2 quarter circles. Glue 1 quarter circle to each corner (illustration B).

B. Add a gold foil monogram and corner trim.

3. **Fill pouch.** Insert dried petals or herbs in pouch, arranging evenly; allow ⅛ cup for every 25-square-inch area (5" x 5") (illustration C). Glue opening closed.

C. Fill the sachet and glue the fourth side closed. Affix Velcro to sachet and drawer corners.

4. **Add Velcro.** Using scissors, cut Velcro into two 1" squares; cut each square in half diagonally. Affix hook triangles to back of pouch at each corner (top left corner of illustration C). Affix loop triangles to drawer floor at corners. Set liner in drawer and press down on corners to adhere.

Gilt SCALLOP SHELL TRAY

By Lily Franklin

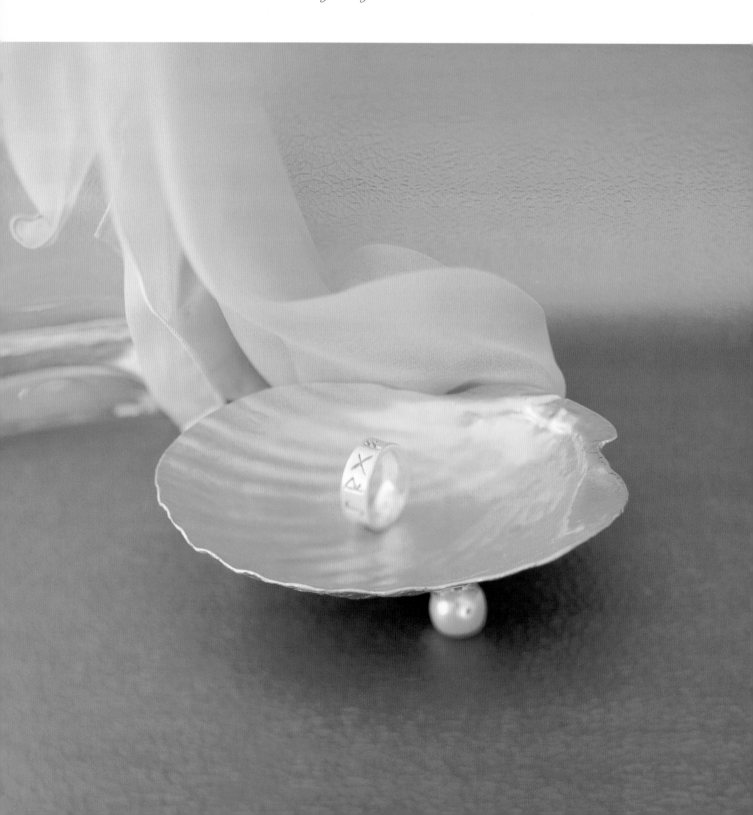

Transform a simple shell into a miniature decorative tray or soap dish for a powder room or bathroom. The smooth, lustrous, gold interior surface contrasts with the textured silver of the rough underside. Three oversized faceted pearls serve as elegant feet.

The gold-colored leaf, actually composed of brass, will tarnish or turn green if exposed directly to acidic items like soap, but a protective finish of epoxy applied under and over the gold leaf prevents direct contact. The inner surface of the shell can be directly leafed, but I found that applying epoxy as a base under the leaf yielded a liquid gold surface that resembled mercury.

Epoxy is a two-part compound that yields a thick, resinous finish with just one coat. Make sure to spread the epoxy over the outer edge to provide a complete seal. Though the epoxy finish is nontoxic after it dries, the shell should not be used to hold foods.

Though many types of shells can be used for this project, a scallop is the most suitable since it is flat and wide. If you don't already have one, scallop shells, also called pectens, can be found for as little as $1 or $2 apiece.

Materials

MAKES 1 SHELL TRAY

5" to 6" scallop shell
Several large baroque pearls in various sizes (you will use 3)
5-minute epoxy
Epoxy sealer
Gold size
Gold composition leaf
Silver composition leaf

You'll also need:

220- and 600-grit wet/dry emery paper, ¼" masking tape, scrap cardboard, toothpicks or small craft sticks, small disposable plastic cup, 2 disposable ¾" bristle brushes, medium-sized bowl, newsprint, mineral spirits (to clean size from brush), 1 sheet white paper, cotton balls, rubbing alcohol

Instructions

1. **Prepare shell surface.** Rub both sides of shell with moist 220-grit emery paper to smooth gritty areas. Sand down sharp rim until blunt.

2. **Attach pearl feet.** Tape 3 pearls to outer shell—2 near front edge and 1 near hinge. Test balance; shell should not touch tabletop and dish should be level. Adjust or substitute pearls as needed (I used a smaller pearl near the hinge). Mix 5-minute epoxy on scrap cardboard with toothpick; let set until no longer runny. Affix 2 front pearls first and then rear pearl (illustration A). Stand upright and let dry 15 minutes.

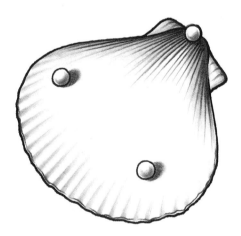

A. Glue 3 pearl feet to the outer shell.

3. **Seal shell surface.** Following manufacturer's instructions, mix 1 teaspoon epoxy sealer in disposable cup. Brush light coat onto inner shell and rim (illustration B). Blow gently across surface to dissipate tiny bubbles. Set in well-ventilated place and cover with overturned bowl

to keep off dust. Let cure 24 hours or until hard. Remove specks and lint using moistened 600-grit emery paper or your fingertip.

B. Coat the inner shell with epoxy sealer.

4. **Apply gold and silver leaf.** Lay newsprint on work surface. Brush thin coat of size on inner shell and rim; tilt shell to prevent pooling. Clean brush with mineral spirits. When size reaches tack (1 to 3 hours), transfer gold leaf sheet to white paper. Tear into irregular 1" pieces. Apply leaf to shell surface and tamp down with brush to gild entire inner shell and rim (illustration C). Let dry 24 hours. Buff lightly with cotton ball. Remove fingerprints using cotton ball moistened with rubbing alcohol. Seal gilded area, as in step 3. After sealer dries, coat outer shell with silver leaf, avoiding legs and rim; do not seal.

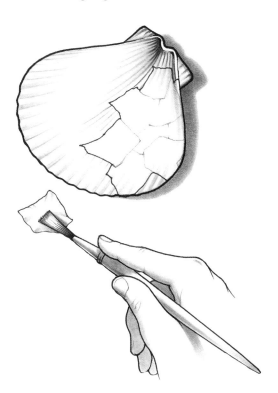

C. Leaf the inner shell gold and the outer shell silver.

Trimmed BATH MAT

By Genevieve A. Sterbenz

Transform an ordinary towel into a whimsical bath mat using trims in an assortment of colors and patterns. Here, a piqué towel with characteristic puckered texture features checkered ribbon around its perimeter and pink grosgrain twirled into the word "bath" in the center. Petite rosebud appliqués are used as accents.

The piqué bath towel I found was a perfect choice for a bath mat. It was constructed from two kinds of fabric: a turquoise piqué on one side and an absorbent turquoise terry cloth on the other. Because the piqué has an interesting and beautiful texture, I used that side for the front of the bath mat. If you cannot find a similar towel, you could simply cut a 24" x 36" rectangle from piqué fabric and back it with a piece of terry cloth cut to the same size. Simply place the fabrics right sides together and stitch 1/4" from all edges, leaving an opening for turning. Then turn right side out and stitch the opening closed.

I used a decorative pink and black checkerboard ribbon trim for the two borders and a flat pink grosgrain ribbon to create the word "bath." Both trims are made from cotton or polyester so they can be easily washed. The trims are bright and beautiful to complement the turquoise, but are also flat so the bath mat will not be uncomfortable when stepped on.

To create the word "bath," I pinned the ribbon first to secure it in place. The squares of the piqué towel make it easy to center the word and check the alignment of the letters to assure uniformity in height and length. I arched the ribbon for the wider letters and folded it over itself for sharp turns or to change directions. If you choose a ribbon that is 1/4" or narrower, machine stitching down the center of the ribbon should be sufficient to secure it to the towel. For a wider ribbon, stitch both edges. To accent and finish the mat, I hand stitched small, flat floral appliqués in a coordinating color to the word "bath."

This is such a fun and simple project, you may consider making coordinating bath and hand towels, as well.

Materials

Piqué bath towel in turquoise, 23" x 35"

Trims from Mokuba:

5⅜ yards ribbon in pink checkerboard pattern, ⅝"-wide

3¼ yards grosgrain ribbon in pink, ¼"-wide

16 appliqué flowers with leaves in pink, 1" x ½"

Thread to match fabric and trims

YOU'LL ALSO NEED:

Pins, clear acrylic grid ruler, sewing machine, pattern (see page 74), scissors, dressmaker's tracing paper, tracing wheel, hand-sewing needle

Instructions

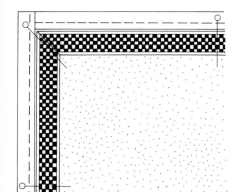

A. Pin ribbon border to outer edge of towel, mitering ribbon at corners.

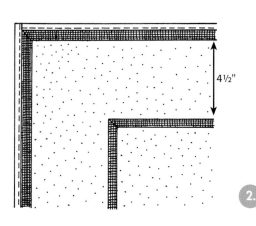

B. Stitch inner ribbon border in place 4½" inside outer border.

1. **Position and stitch down checkerboard ribbon for outside and inside borders.** Lay towel on clean, flat work surface, right side up. Smooth flat with hands. Position and pin checkerboard ribbon to outer edge of towel, aligning one long edge of ribbon with inner edge of hem. (If your towel does not have a hem on all sides, position ribbon an even distance from the edge on all sides.) Fold ribbon back on itself at corner, and then bring ribbon back down parallel with adjacent side and pin, forming a mitered corner (illustration A).

   Continue pinning around remaining 3 sides and squaring corners in the same manner. Overlap ends by ¾" and turn under raw edge. Edgestitch one edge of ribbon to towel, removing pins as you work. Then repeat for opposite edge, sewing in same direction around towel. Position and pin a second border of checkerboard ribbon around towel in the same manner as for the outside border, positioning outer edge of ribbon 4½" from inner edge of outer ribbon border. Stitch in place as for previous ribbon border (illustration B).

2. **Position and stitch down "bath" ribbon.** Photocopy lettering pattern on page 74, enlarging 167%. Transfer pattern to center of towel, using tracing paper and tracing wheel. Pin ribbon along the short line of the letter "a," between small dots, trimming excess; stitch down

center of ribbon or along both edges to secure in place. Cut a clean edge and make a knot 1" from one end of grosgrain ribbon. Position knotted end at lower left of transferred lettering on marked line starting at letter "b"; pin. Continue pinning ribbon to marked lines, turning ribbon around loose curves and folding ribbon over itself at sharp turns, such as at top of "a." Cut ribbon on right side of letter "a," where lines intersect, as shown. Stitch pinned ribbon in place, breaking thread and backstitching at knot and removing pins as you come to them (illustration C).

Detail

C. Stitch ribbon over marked lines for letters "b" and "a" as shown.

Pin remaining ribbon in a continuous line, along remaining pattern lines, from the top of the letter "a" through the letter "h," with the exception of the line that crosses the top of the "t." Lap ribbon over cut ribbon edge on the right side of the letter "a" to conceal the raw edge and tie a knot in ribbon at a point 1" from the end of the marked line for the letter "h"; trim excess. Note that the raw cut edge of the ribbon at the top of the letter "a" will be concealed in step 3 with a flower appliqué. Stitch ribbon in place, breaking stitching and backstitching on each side of the knot. Tie a knot 1" from the end of the remaining length of ribbon. Pin ribbon to the marked line that crosses the letter "t," tying a second knot 1" from the end of the marked line; trim excess. Stitch ribbon in place, breaking stitching and backstitching on each side of the knots.

3 **Finishing.** Handstitch appliqué flowers with leaves in place at the large marked dots, using the pattern as a guide for placement. Stitch only through first layer of fabric.

Lettering Pattern
Photocopy at 167%.

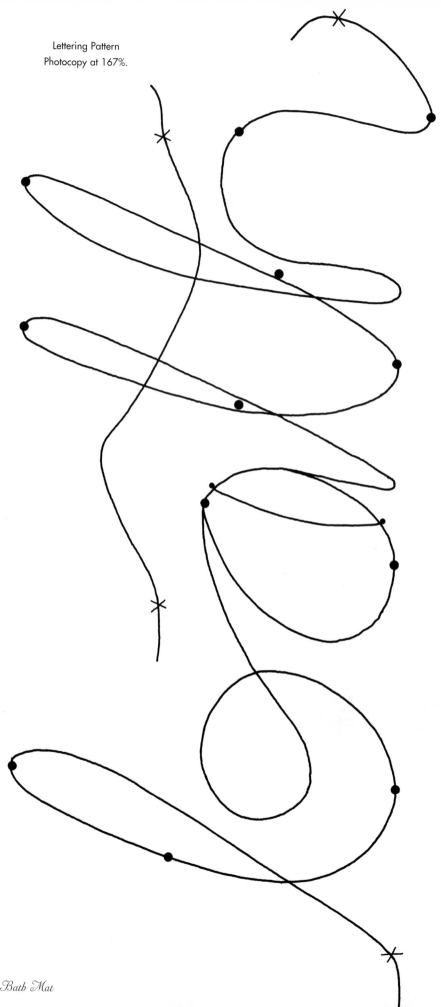

BEADED WASTEBASKET

By Elizabeth Cameron

Cover a wire wastebasket with beads using a simple wrap-and-trap technique. Start by stringing the beads one by one onto a wire and trapping them in place by wrapping a second, thinner gauge wire around the original wire and bead. The strand of beaded wire is then wound around the belly of the wastebasket.

I like the look of translucent glass beads because of the way they reflect the light. I chose a variety of bead styles, including doughnut shapes in shades of turquoise, lime, and royal blue. For a similar look using other colors, choose beads that are next to each other on the color wheel. Instead of the cool tones I chose, try combining warm reds with hot pink and orange tones.

Materials

MAKES 1 WASTEBASKET

20-gauge silver spool wire
24-gauge silver spool wire
Assorted glass beads in a variety of sizes
Glass doughnuts
Wire wastebasket

YOU'LL ALSO NEED:

Large paint can or basketball, wire cutters

Instructions

1. **String beads.** Wrap 20-gauge wire 5 or 6 times around a basketball or large paint can, add 2", and clip with wire cutters. Unwind 10" of 24-gauge wire from a spool, but do not cut. Hold the 2 wire ends together, and twist the 24-gauge wire around the 20-gauge wire 2 or 3 times, for a spiral about ½" long. Slip the first bead onto the 20-gauge wire and slide it down to the spiraled section. To lock the bead in place, twist the 24-gauge wire around the 20-gauge wire 2 or 3 times. Repeat

the process with additional beads until you reach the end of the 20-gauge wire (illustration A).

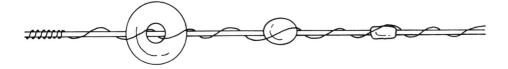

A. String beads on 20-gauge wire and secure in place by wrapping with a 24-gauge wire.

To end off, spiral the 24-gauge wire around the 20-gauge wire for ½", then clip the wire from the spool. Create a second beaded wire of about the same length.

2. Secure beaded wire to basket. Wind the twined ends of a beaded wire around a vertical support on the wastebasket. Cut a length of 24-gauge wire equal to the height of the wastebasket, plus 4" for each vertical support. Anchor the 24-gauge wires at the top of each vertical support. Wind the beaded wire around the wastebasket. Weave the 24-gauge wire over and under the wire rings of the vertical supports, securing the beaded wire as it passes each vertical support (illustration B).

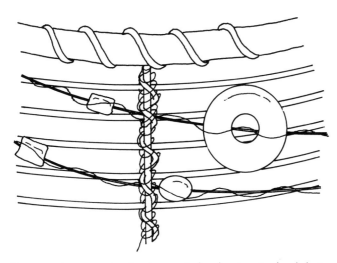

B. Wrap 24-gauge wire over and under along vertical spokes, trapping beaded wires in place.

RESOURCES

American Science and Surplus
847-982-0870
www.sciplus.com
Glass bottles and corks
(Beach Breeze Body Lotion, page 14)

Beads and Beyond
25 102nd Avenue NE
Bellevue, WA 98004
425-462-8992
Hollow glass beads, bead caps, assorted beads, hat pins, glass doughnuts
(Blown Glass Bottle Stoppers, page 59;
Beaded Wastebasket, page 75)

Bear America Sales
PO Box 829
Bear, DE 19701-0829
Tlshay@magpage.com
soapsupplies.freeyellow.com
Coconut oil
(Handmade Soap, page 8)

Cedarbrook Herb Farm
1345 Sequim Avenue S.
Sequim, WA 98382
360-683-7733
888-811-5442
www.lavenderfarms.com/cedarbrook
"Moth-Be-Gone" moth repellent herbs
(Padded Scented Hanger, page 52)

Jell-O Mold Offer
P.O. Box 390351
El Paso, TX 88539-0351
www.kraftfoods.com/jell-o/
Egg-shaped mold
(Aromatic Egg Soaps, page 25)

Lavender Lane
7337 Roseville Road, Suite #1
Sacramento, CA 95842
888-593-4400
healthychoices@lavenderlane.com
www.lavenderlane.com
Natural essential oils, carrier oils, small round tins (#LTIN)
(Fragrant Bath Tablets, page 5; Lip Balm, page 18)

Mokuba New York
55 West 39th Street
New York, NY 10018
212-869-8900
Decorative trims
(Envelope Slipcover for a Bath Pillow, page 40; Padded Scented Hanger, page 52; Trimmed Bath Mat, page 70)

Pearl Paint Company, Inc.
308 Canal Street
New York, NY 10013-2572
800-451-PEARL (catalog)
www.pearlpaint.com
French Corner labels and Creative Beginnings charms
(Beach Breeze Body Lotion, page 14)

Rainbow Meadow, Inc.
P.O. Box 457
Napoleon, MI 49261
800-207-4047
517-817-0021
fax 800-219-0213
www.rainbowmeadow.com
Essential oils, melt and pour soap base, and carrier oils
(Beach Breeze Body Lotion, page 14)

Simple Pleasures
P.O. Box 194
Old Saybrook, CT 06475
pigmntlady@aol.com
http://members.aol.com/pigmntlady/
Pigments
(Lip Balm, page 18)

Sugar Plum Sundries
1106 McCallie Avenue
Chattanooga, TN 37404
423-624-4511
www.mindspring.com/~sugarplum/main.htm
Lye
(Handmade Soap, page 8)

SunFeather Natural Soap Company
1551 State Highway 72
Potsdam, NY 13676
800-771-7627
315-265-3648
www.sunsoap.com
Essential and fragrance oils and coconut oil
(Handmade Soap, page 8)

Sweet Cakes Soapmaking Supplies
249 North Road
Kinnelon, NJ 07405
973-838-5200
www.sweetcakes.com
Fragrances and glycerine soap base
(Beach Breeze Body Lotion, page 14; Lip Balm, page 18; Aromatic Egg Soaps, page 25)

TKB Trading
356 24th St.
Oakland, CA 94612
510-451-9011
www.tkbtrading.com
Glycerin melt-and-pour soap, cosmetic-grade colorants, cosmetic-grade glitter and sparkle powder, fragrance oil, including champagne-scented fragrance oil
(Champagne and Confetti Loaf Soaps, page 29)

CONTRIBUTORS

All color photography by Carl Tremblay, except as noted.

Fragrant Bath Tablets
DESIGNER: *Amy Jenner*
ILLUSTRATOR: *Jil Johänson*

Handmade Soap
DESIGNER: *Amy Jenner*
ILLUSTRATOR: *Nenad Jakesevic*

Beach Breeze Body Lotion
DESIGNER: *Mary Ann Hall*
ILLUSTRATOR: *Jil Johänson*

Lip Balm
DESIGNER: *Mary Ann Hall*
ILLUSTRATOR: *Mary Newell DePalma*

Aromatic Egg Soaps
DESIGNER: *Lily Franklin*
ILLUSTRATOR: *Jil Johänson*

Champagne and Confetti Loaf Soaps
DESIGNER: *Kaila Westerman*
ILLUSTRATOR: *Jil Johänson*

Polka Dot Soap Dish and Tumbler
DESIGNER: *Genevieve A. Sterbenz*
ILLUSTRATOR: *Jil Johänson*
PHOTOGRAPHER: *Bill Lindner*

Daisy Shower Curtain
DESIGNER: *Dawn Anderson*
ILLUSTRATOR: *Jil Johänson*

Envelope Slipcover for a Bath Pillow
DESIGNER: *Genevieve A. Sterbenz*
ILLUSTRATOR: *Jil Johänson*
PHOTOGRAPHER: *Bill Lindner*

Painted Mini-Chest
DESIGNER: *Dawn Anderson*
ILLUSTRATOR: *Jil Johänson*

Embellished Hand Towels
DESIGNER: *Genevieve A. Sterbenz*
ILLUSTRATOR: *Jil Johänson*
PHOTOGRAPHER: *Bill Lindner*

Padded Scented Hanger
DESIGNER: *Dawn Anderson*
ILLUSTRATORS: *Mary Newell DePalma and Roberta Frauwirth*

Blown Glass Bottle Stoppers
DESIGNER: *Dawn Anderson*
ILLUSTRATOR: *Judy Love*

Drawer-Liner Sachets
DESIGNER: *Elizabeth Cameron*
ILLUSTRATOR: *Michael Gellatly*

Gilt Scallop Shell Tray
DESIGNER: *Lily Franklin*
ILLUSTRATOR: *Michael Gellatly*

Trimmed Bath Mat
DESIGNER: *Genevieve A. Sterbenz*
ILLUSTRATOR: *Jil Johänson*
PHOTOGRAPHER: *Bill Lindner*

Beaded Wastebasket
DESIGNER: *Elizabeth Cameron*
ILLUSTRATOR: *Jil Johänson*